Symbols of America

THE STATUE OF LIBERTY

by Cari Meister

PEBBLE
a capstone imprint

Published by Pebble, an imprint of Capstone
1710 Roe Crest Drive, North Mankato, Minnesota 56003
capstonepub.com

Library of Congress Cataloging-in-Publication Data is available on the Library of Congress website.

ISBN: 9798875248214 (hardcover)
ISBN: 9798875248160 (paperback)
ISBN: 9798875248177 (ebook PDF)

Summary: Simple text introduces readers to the Statue of Liberty, explaining its history, meaning, and why it is an important symbol today.

Editorial Credits
Editor: Mandy Robbins; Designer: Sarah Bennett; Media Researcher: Rebekah Hubstenberger; Production Specialist: Tori Abraham

Image Credits
Getty Images: Bill Ross, 7, Bryan Bedder, 20, Graphic House, 9, iStock/OlegAlbinsky, 8, 19, Richard Hamilton Smith, 17, Tetra Images, 5, Three Lions, 15, Yukinori Hasumi, 4; Library of Congress: Prints & Photographs Division, 12; Newscom: Nps/ZUMA Press, 11; Shutterstock: ANNA DOMINIKA (watercolor background), back cover and throughout, Dragon Images, 21, Elena_Suvorova, 18, Francisco Javier Gil, 16, Sergii Figurnyi, front cover

Printed and bound in China. 006460

Table of Contents

Words in **bold** are in the glossary

A Special Welcome

Look at the big green lady in New York **Harbor**! She is the Statue of Liberty. She stands on a tiny island. The statue holds up a **torch** to welcome people.

Lady Liberty wears a crown with seven points. Each point stands for a **continent**. The points look like rays of light.

Lady Liberty is very big! She stands on a high **pedestal**. Together, they are 305 feet and 1 inch (93 meters) tall. Her feet are 25 feet (7.6 m) long. If she wore shoes, they would be size 879!

The Story of Our Statue

The Statue of Liberty was a gift from the French. France gave this big gift after the United States ended **enslavement**. It showed that our countries shared **values**. Both nations cared about freedom and equality.

A man named Frederic Bartholdi **designed** the statue. He based the statue's face on his mother's face.

Lady Liberty came on a big ship. But she was too big to be brought over whole. First, she had to be taken apart in France. Her parts were carefully wrapped and shipped in 214 giant wooden crates.

When the ship arrived in New York, workers unpacked the crates. The statue was like a giant puzzle. Workers spent months putting her pieces together. They had to climb very high to reach the top parts.

What the Statue Means

People from other countries have come to the United States looking for better lives. The Statue of Liberty was the first thing those who sailed into New York saw. Lady Liberty made them feel hopeful. Her torch showed them the way to a free land.

Lady Liberty holds a book. The book shows a special date. It is July 4, 1776. That is the birthday of the United States.

Look at her feet. She has broken chains. The chains are broken to show the United States is the land of the free.

Our Statue Today

The Statue of Liberty was not always green. She was once shiny copper, like a new penny. Rain, air, and **pollution** made her turn green.

At night, lights make her glow. She looks like a giant night-light. She watches over New York Harbor.

Many people visit the Statue of Liberty. Some climb up to her crown. Nearby, there is a museum. You can learn many more facts about her there.

Make Your Own Statue!

Get out some modeling clay and make your own statue. What will it be? Make it something you care about. What does it mean to you?

Glossary

continent (KAHN-tuh-nuhnt)—one of Earth's seven large land masses

design (di-ZYN)—to make a plan for how to build something

enslavement (en-SLAYV-muhnt)—the owning of other people; enslaved people worked without pay

harbor (HAR-bur)—a place where ships load and unload passengers and cargo

pedestal (PEH-duh-stuhl)—a base that something stands on

pollution (puh-LOO-shuhn)—materials that hurt Earth's water, air, and land

torch (TORCH)—a portable device that gives light

value (VAL-yoo)—a belief or idea that is important to people

Can You Remember?

1. What does the statue hold in her hands?
2. Which country gave us the statue?
3. What color was the statue when it was new?
4. How many points are on her crown?

Index

About the Author

Cari Meister lives in Vail, Colorado, with her family and rescue dog. Cari is a children's librarian and the author of more than 300 books. She enjoys reading, skiing, yoga, running, and riding her horse, Sir William.